All About America

COWBOYS AND THE WILD WEST

Hilarie N. Staton

KINGFISHER

NEW YORK

All About America: COWBOYS AND THE WILD WEST

KINGFISHER
LONDON & NEW YORK

Copyright © Bender Richardson White 2011

Published in the United States by Kingfisher,
175 Fifth Ave., New York, NY 10010
Kingfisher is an imprint of Macmillan Children's Books, London.
All rights reserved.

Distributed in the U.S. by Macmillan, 175 Fifth Ave.,
New York, NY 10010
Distributed in Canada by H.B. Fenn and Company Ltd.,
34 Nixon Road, Bolton, Ontario L7E 1W2

Library of Congress Cataloging-in-Publication data has been applied for.

ISBN paperback 978-0-7534-6510-3
ISBN reinforced library binding 978-0-7534-6582-0

Kingfisher books are available for special promotions and premiums. For details contact: Special Markets Department, Macmillan, 175 Fifth Ave., New York, NY 10010.

For more information, please visit www.kingfisherbooks.com

Printed in China
10 9 8 7 6 5 4 3 2 1
1TR/0311/WKT/UNTD/140MA

The All About America series was produced for Kingfisher by Bender Richardson White, Uxbridge, U.K.
Editor: Lionel Bender
Designer: Ben White
DTP: Neil Sutton
Production: Kim Richardson
Consultant: Richard Jensen, Research Professor of History, Culver Stockton College, Missouri

Sources of quotations and excerpts

Pages 5, 10, 11, 15, 21, 26, 28: interview quotes in Library of Congress: American Life Histories: Manuscripts from the Federal Writer's Project, 1936–1940.
Page 8: Ranching profits quote: Thayer, William Makepeace. *Marvels of the New West*, p. 547. Norwich, CT: The Henry Bill Publishing Company, 1890.
Page 12: W. H. Thomas Quote: Slatta, Richard W. *Cowboy: The Illustrated History*, p. 19. Sterling, 2006.
Pages 16, 18: song lyrics in *Cowboy Songs and Other Frontier Ballads*, p. 10. Collected by John A. Lomax and Alan Lomax. NY: The Macmillan Company, 1938.
Page 19: stampede and rustlers quotes: Abbott, E. C. "Teddy Blue" and Helena Huntington Smith. *We Pointed Them North, Recollections of a Cowpuncher*, pp. 66, 70. Chicago, IL: R. R. Donnelley & Sons Company, 1991.
Page 23: Dubbs: Dodge City quote: Goodnight, Charles, Emanuel Dubbs, John A. Hart, and others. *Pioneer Days in the Southwest, From 1850–1879*, p. 35. Guthrie, OK: The State Capital Company, 1909.
Page 24: Wild Bill Hickok quote: Harger, Charles Moreau. "Cattle Trails of the Prairie." *Scribner's Magazine*, volume 11, issue 6, June, 1892.
Page 25: Elfego Baca quote: Smith, Janet. Interview with Elfego Baca, p.1. New Mexico: July 13, 1936.

Acknowledgments

The publishers would like to thank the following illustrators for their contribution to this book: Richard Berridge, Christian Hook, and John James. Map: Neil Sutton. Book cover design: Michael Yuen.
Cover artwork: John James.
The publishers thank the following for supplying photos for this book: b = bottom, c = center, l = left, t = top, m = middle: © The Art Archive: pages 18t (The Art Archive/Bill Manns) • © The Bridgeman Art Library: Peter Newark Western Americana pages 8t, 18m; 13t (Hogg Brothers Collection, Gift of Miss Ima Hogg); 17t (Christie's Images); 26bl (Peter Newark American Pictures); 26 (Peter Newark Pictures); 28l (Peter Newark American Pictures) • © Dorling Kindersley: pages 6t (Geoff Brightling); 19 (Frank Greenaway); 20t and cover (Geoff Brightling) • © istockphoto.com: pages 8–9b (Dale Reardon); 10ml (Manuel Velasco); 10bl (Stanley Lange); 16t (DNY59); 19t (Robert Kohlhuber); 22tl (Don Nichols); 23tl (Renee Lee); 26–27 (Vladimir Maravic); 28tl (Milos Luzanin); 29mr (Kriss Russell) • © Library of Congress: pages 1c and cover (LC-DIG-ppmsca-17869); 1, 2–3, 30–31, 32 (LC-DIG-ppmsc-02629); 4b (LC-DIG-ppmsc-08795); 7tl (LC-DIG-pga-03118); 8–9m (LC-DIG-pga-01454); 10t (LC-DIG-ppmsca-17998); 10b (LC-DIG-ppmsc-02632); 12–13 (LC-DIG-ppmsca-08791); 15b (LC-USZ62-56646); 16 (LC-DIG-ppmsc-02638); 29tl (LC-USZC4-8945); 29ml (LC-USZC4-2740) • © Sears Roebuck: page 27r • © www.shutterstock.com: pages 12tl (Sascha Burkard); 12–13 (Olivier Le Queinec); 14t (Mike Flippo); 22m (CreativeHQ); 22bl (CreativeHQ); 23tr and cover (CreativeHQ); 22tr (J. Helgason); 22hr (Bryan Sikora) • © TopFoto.co.uk: Topham Picturepoint page 4; The Granger Collection/TopFoto pages 5, 6tr, 7tl, 6–7, 7bl, 7mr, 8bl, 9tl, 14–15, 15t, 16bl, 18b, 20m, 21t, 21m, 22bm and cover, 23–23, 25, 29bl; World History Archive/TopFoto page 23m.
Every effort has been made to trace the copyright holders of the images. The publishers apologize for any omissions.

Note to readers: The website addresses listed in this book are correct at the time of publishing. However, due to the ever-changing nature of the Internet, website addresses and content can change. Websites can contain links that are unsuitable for children. The publisher cannot be held responsible for changes in website addresses or content, or for information obtained through third-party websites. We strongly advise that Internet searches should be supervised by an adult.

CONTENTS

Introduction

Cowboys and the Wild West looks at an exciting part of everyday life in America from the early 1800s to around 1890. It focuses on how Spanish pioneers brought cattle from Mexico to Texas and set up ranches. Other pioneers built ranches, too. The men who took care of the cattle and horses were cowboys. The story is presented as a series of double-page articles, each one looking at a particular topic, including how cowboys worked, lived, enjoyed themselves—and got into trouble. It is illustrated with paintings, engravings, and photographs from the time, mixed with artists' impressions of everyday scenes and situations.

Cowboy Country

Cattle roaming wild and then moved to market

The story of cowboys and western ranches is one of the open range, panicky cattle, horse-riding skills, and railroads. It is about the trip cowboys and cattle took together over long, dangerous trails and the legacies that cowboys have left us.

Clearing the Plains of Buffalo

Vast herds of buffalo, or American bison, covered the plains until the 1870s. Then these huge animals were hunted for their skins, which were used for blankets and leather clothing and to make belts for machines. By the mid-1880s, the buffalo were gone from the range.

Before Spanish settlers arrived, much of Texas was empty grassland area. Where the weather was mostly dry, the grass was short and scrubby. In wetter areas, the grass was tall and lush, and streams and rivers cut across the flat prairie and rolling hills. Grasslands reached all the way north into Canada, and the main grazing animal was the mighty buffalo. This land turned out to be perfect for grazing cattle.

Getting cattle to market for profit

In 1521, the Spanish brought a few cattle to Texas. Ranchers let their cattle run free on Texas's open range. These cattle became the Texas longhorns, which survived and thrived. Cowboys gathered the ranchers' herds only when they needed to use them. Yet there were more cattle than the people nearby needed for meat, hides, or tallow. When the railroads came to the plains in the 1870s, ranchers realized they could ship their cattle to stockyards and slaughter houses in big cities and make a profit. They just had to round up the cattle and get them to the railroads.

▶ Cowboys spent most of their time with the cattle. The main breed of cattle, the Texas longhorn, had huge horns, was stubborn, and got scared easily but could survive for days without water.

▲ Cattle included the young (calves and heifers), adult females (cows), adult males for mating (bulls), and other adult males (steers).

◄ This map shows the cattle trails from Texas's open range to the railroads, hundreds of miles north. Leading the cattle along a trail was a dangerous trip, but once the cattle were loaded into railroad cars, the cowboys celebrated.

CANADA

N

Kansas City
Abilene
Sedalia
St. Louis
Dodge City
San Antonio

MEXICO

GOODNIGHT – LOVING TRAIL
WESTERN TRAIL
CHISHOLM TRAIL
OLD SHAWNEE TRAIL

Longhorn
Shorthorn
Brahman
Hereford

Texas Cattle

The cattle brought by the Spanish settlers adapted and produced the Texas longhorn. After 1850, Texas ranchers brought shorthorns and brown-and-white Herefords from England, and the all-white Brahman from India. Ranchers mixed these breeds to develop healthy, fast-growing cattle that provided good meat.

The golden era of the cowboy

During the main cowboy period, from 1867 until the 1880s, cattle drives went from Texas to railroad towns in Kansas. Being on a drive involved hard, dirty, lonely, and low-paid work, and there were dangers from cattle stampedes and outlaws. Work on a ranch was only a little easier. Sometimes after being on the range or trail, cowboys might celebrate too much, but most had a strong code of honor. The era ended when settlers fenced in the land, railroads expanded, and years of storms killed cattle. Today, cowboys are still working with cattle, using many of the same methods.

As the drives ended, writers and showmen told stories about cowboy life. The stories and movies made about them pictured an exciting life for cowboys, lawmen, rustlers, and outlaws. However, L. M. Cox, a real cowboy, said, "The cowboy's life as we know it was certainly lacking in the glamour which we see on our screens today."

Opening New Markets

In May 1869, railroads from the East and West coasts joined. The new railroads provided a way for ranchers to get their cattle to profitable big city markets. First, though, thousands of cattle from Texas's open range had to be moved to the railroads.

Vaqueros

Skilled horsemen from Mexico

Christopher Columbus brought horses and cattle to the Americas. Later, *vaqueros* used techniques from Spain to care for the cattle, and settlers learned these skills from them.

▲ A cowboy's leather *tapaderas*, or stirrup covers, to protect his feet from the weather

Soldiers, missionaries, and settlers from Spain brought live animals with them on their ships. In Mexico, some cattle and horses escaped and formed wild herds. The animals were free to anyone who could catch and manage them. Some of the Spanish settlers became very skilled at riding horses and roping cattle. These men became known as *vaqueros*, which is a Spanish word for cowboys. On farms, or ranches, they helped raise the cattle, which were used for meat, hides, and tallow. Hides are tanned animal skins that are made into leather for clothes, boots, saddles, and harnesses. Tallow is fat that is boiled down and used to make soap and candles. Ranches sold their cattle, often to the missions or to feed soldiers.

▼ The escaped Spanish cattle roamed free in Texas and slowly adapted to the local conditions. Within a few generations, they had formed a new breed, the Texas longhorns.

▲ *Vaqueros* adapted Spanish skills and equipment to work with cattle in the Americas. This *vaquero*'s saddle, spurs, lariat, and leather chaps were similar to those that were used in Spain.

6

◀ *Vaqueros* and other cowboys rode the range, rounded up wild cattle, and branded them.

Fancy but Practical

Vaqueros wore fancy clothes that were just as practical as the working clothes of later cowboys. The wide brim of the *vaquero*'s sombrero and the cowboy's hat kept off the sun and rain. The tall boots and leather chaps protected their legs from horse bites and cacti.

Early ranches and trail drives

In the 1830s, many U.S. citizens moved west to Texas, set up ranches, and learned cowboy skills from the *vaqueros* who were already working there. Nearby, in what is now Oklahoma, American Indians raised cattle, too. They had been forced by the government to move to this area, called Indian Territory. Some had been allowed to bring their cattle, and they became skilled cowboys.

Over the following years, the number of cattle grew. Ranchers hired cowboys to round up their cattle, and some sent small herds to New Orleans or the Texas Gulf Coast to breed on ranches there or to be shipped to other places. In 1846, the first long cattle drive went from Texas to Ohio. The drive was hard on the animals and cowboys. The cattle lost weight and were very thin when they arrived. Then, in 1861, the Civil War began. Texas joined the South, and many cowboys left to enlist in the Confederate army. At first cattle were sent to feed Confederate soldiers, but then the Union army blocked the Mississippi River, so the cattle could not reach the Confederates. Without *vaqueros* and other cowboys to care for them, the cattle were left alone on the open range.

▶ In California, American Indians were trained to be *vaqueros* for the Spanish missions.

Catching Mustangs

When Spanish horses escaped, they formed wild herds. These horses were called mustangs. Mustangs were prized by both American Indians, such as the Comanche, and cowboys. Riders valued the endurance and speed of these small horses. But some could not be tamed.

The Cattle Business
Getting rich by feeding the nation

An 1890 book, *Marvels of the New West*, states: "The profits of stock-raising are marvelous. For this reason, men endure hardships and brave dangers, dwelling apart from friends and civilized society."

Ranchers returned to Texas after the Civil War to find their ranches falling apart. Some six million cattle were running wild on the Texas range, but there was no place nearby to sell them. In 1866, Charles Goodnight rounded up around 2,000 head of cattle and traveled west to New Mexico and Colorado. He sold his cattle at a big profit. The next year, Joseph McCoy built a stockyard near the Abilene, Kansas, railroad station. He encouraged ranchers to bring their cattle to his stockyard, where buyers bought the cattle and shipped them east by rail. At first, companies shipped live cattle to the East. Then, using new technology, the meatpacking industry shipped fresh meat, canned meat, and other products.

Cattle Barons

The men who owned the biggest ranches, had the most power, and made the most money were called cattle barons. Those pictured above started as cowboys, saved all their money, and bought cattle and land until they owned a large ranch. However, Charles Lux began as a California butcher before becoming a cattleman. Before he became president, Teddy Roosevelt invested in a cattle ranch and learned to do a cowboy's job. Other investors only stood and watched cowboys working.

▼ The hard work of raising cattle was done by cowboys.

BEEF & PORK IN PACKAGES SUITABLE FOR FOREIGN & DOMESTIC MARKETS.

HALSTE BEEF & PORK PACKER 194 to 202 New York

8

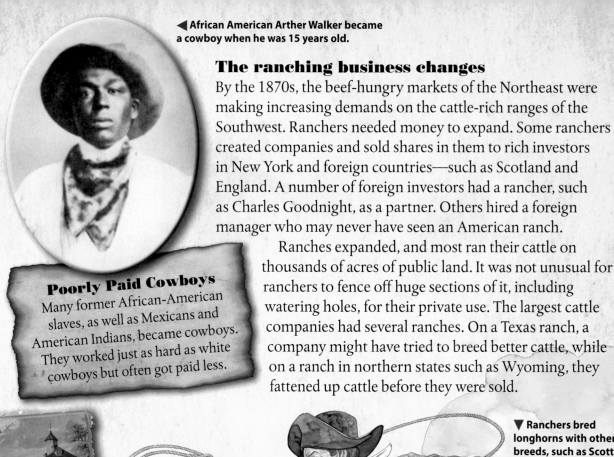

◀ African American Arther Walker became a cowboy when he was 15 years old.

The ranching business changes

By the 1870s, the beef-hungry markets of the Northeast were making increasing demands on the cattle-rich ranges of the Southwest. Ranchers needed money to expand. Some ranchers created companies and sold shares in them to rich investors in New York and foreign countries—such as Scotland and England. A number of foreign investors had a rancher, such as Charles Goodnight, as a partner. Others hired a foreign manager who may never have seen an American ranch.

Ranches expanded, and most ran their cattle on thousands of acres of public land. It was not unusual for ranchers to fence off huge sections of it, including watering holes, for their private use. The largest cattle companies had several ranches. On a Texas ranch, a company might have tried to breed better cattle, while on a ranch in northern states such as Wyoming, they fattened up cattle before they were sold.

Poorly Paid Cowboys

Many former African-American slaves, as well as Mexicans and American Indians, became cowboys. They worked just as hard as white cowboys but often got paid less.

▼ Ranchers bred longhorns with other breeds, such as Scottish shorthorn cattle. The new breeds were not as nervous as Texas longhorns.

◀ Live animals were sent by rail to slaughter houses, where they were killed and their meat sold to butchers.

◀ A cowboy jingled when he walked because of the chains that helped hold his spurs on to his boots.

On the Ranch

Work to be done all year round

On a ranch, everyone had jobs to do to keep the place running smoothly. The rancher, his family, and his cowboys were always busy and worked hard.

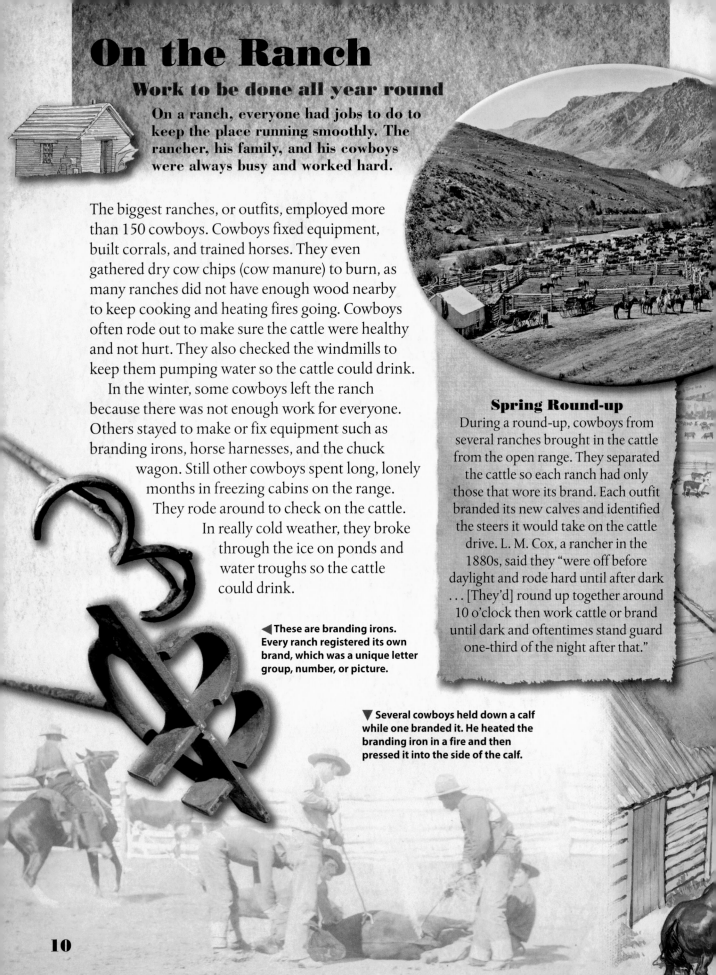

The biggest ranches, or outfits, employed more than 150 cowboys. Cowboys fixed equipment, built corrals, and trained horses. They even gathered dry cow chips (cow manure) to burn, as many ranches did not have enough wood nearby to keep cooking and heating fires going. Cowboys often rode out to make sure the cattle were healthy and not hurt. They also checked the windmills to keep them pumping water so the cattle could drink.

In the winter, some cowboys left the ranch because there was not enough work for everyone. Others stayed to make or fix equipment such as branding irons, horse harnesses, and the chuck wagon. Still other cowboys spent long, lonely months in freezing cabins on the range. They rode around to check on the cattle. In really cold weather, they broke through the ice on ponds and water troughs so the cattle could drink.

◄ These are branding irons. Every ranch registered its own brand, which was a unique letter group, number, or picture.

Spring Round-up

During a round-up, cowboys from several ranches brought in the cattle from the open range. They separated the cattle so each ranch had only those that wore its brand. Each outfit branded its new calves and identified the steers it would take on the cattle drive. L. M. Cox, a rancher in the 1880s, said they "were off before daylight and rode hard until after dark . . . [They'd] round up together around 10 o'clock then work cattle or brand until dark and oftentimes stand guard one-third of the night after that."

▼ Several cowboys held down a calf while one branded it. He heated the branding iron in a fire and then pressed it into the side of the calf.

Women ranchers

Few women lived on ranches, so cowboys were protective of the rancher's wife and daughters. Women might run a ranch because their husbands had died, or because they had taken over the family business. In 1886, Mabel Luke married rancher Jim Madison. "I liked ranch life right from the start, for I rode the range with Jim, learned to cook and eat chuck wagon food and to ride and rope with the best of them. Our cowpunchers were a jolly bunch and always ready for a good time. We got lots of fun out of rodeos, chuck suppers, roping contests and dances. Our ranch was the J-M ranch, and our cattle was branded with the J on the shoulder, the bar on the side, and the M on the hip."

Bunkhouse Living

At the ranch, cowboys lived in the bunkhouse. Each had a bed to call his own and a place for his belongings. The cowboys decorated the walls with pictures of loved ones or pictures from magazines or catalogs. But in the summer, the cowboys would sleep outside to escape the bugs, heat, and smells that came from sweaty men.

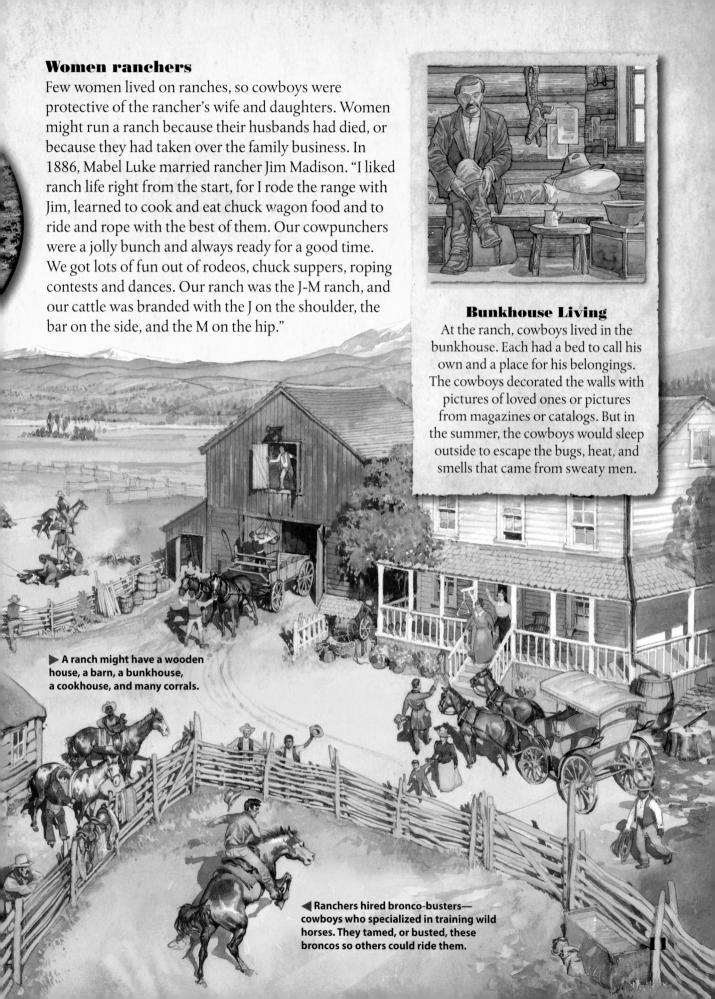

▶ A ranch might have a wooden house, a barn, a bunkhouse, a cookhouse, and many corrals.

◀ Ranchers hired bronco-busters—cowboys who specialized in training wild horses. They tamed, or busted, these broncos so others could ride them.

11

In the Saddle

On horseback daybreak to nightfall

Most cowboys did not own much, but everything they had helped them do their job. Their work was usually done while riding horseback, roping, and caring for the cattle and horses.

A cowboy's hat kept off the sun, rain, and dust. He used it as a scoop to pick up water and to fan over coals to create a flame. He slapped his horse with it to get the animal moving. His bandana—a large handkerchief worn around his neck—kept the dust out of his face in a windstorm and soaked up sweat. His chaps protected his legs. His boots had high tops to protect his legs from rattlesnakes, pointed toes to slip quickly into the stirrup, and high heels to hold his foot in place. One cowboy, W. H. Thomas, said he slept "out under the stars with a slicker for a cover, my saddle blanket for a mattress, my boots under my neck, and my saddle for a pillow."

The horse was critical to a cowboy's job, but most cowboys used a ranch's horses rather than owning their own. A cowboy depended on his horse to stand still while he roped something and to move quickly when danger was near.

▲ A saddle might last a cowboy 30 years.

A Cowboy's Saddle

A leather saddle was a cowboy's most valuable possession. It had to be comfortable, since he spent 12 to 15 hours a day sitting in it. It had a horn with a long neck so a rope could be tied around it. The wide stirrups gave him a sturdy place to stand while staying on the horse.

▲ A cowboy's hat was probably his favorite possession. He used his rope, or lariat, to catch loose cattle or horses, or to pull logs.

◄ In his saddle pack, a cowboy had a slicker—an oiled cotton coat—to put on when it rained, a blanket, and a few biscuits.

A day on the trail

The cookie woke the cowboys very early and soon left, driving his chuck wagon. The wrangler, leading the herd of horses, left next. The cowboys ate breakfast, watered the cattle, and got them moving. On most days, they traveled slowly, about 10 miles (16 km) per day so the cattle would not lose weight. They would travel until they found camp. Cowboys ate cold biscuits and beef jerky while they rode, but when they stopped, the cookie gave them a hot meal.

At night, each cowboy took a four-hour shift guarding the herd. Two cowboys rode around the herd, preventing stampedes and watching for rustlers. Cowboys usually slept in their clothes because they never knew when they might have to rush off to stop a stampede.

▶ *An Angry Cow*—a painting by Olaf Seltzer (1877–1957), a one-time cowboy and railroad worker.

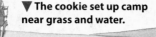

▼ **The cookie set up camp near grass and water.**

▲ **The chuck wagon was a mobile kitchen. In it were stored all the cooking and eating equipment. A large barrel of water was attached to one side of the wagon. The word *chuck* was used locally then to mean food.**

▶ **For dinner, the cowboys usually ate beans, dried pork or beef stew, and biscuits or bread, and they drank lots of very strong, hot coffee. Sometimes, for a treat, the cookie served dried or canned fruit.**

The Chuck Wagon
Charles Goodnight built the first chuck wagon for his 1866 trail drive. Chuck wagons were pulled by horses, oxen, or mules. They had shelves, drawers, and a hinged door that folded down into a table. Food and first-aid supplies, cowboys' bedrolls, and all their personal belongings were stored in the wagon. Every night, it was the center of the camp.

Stampede!

Riding at a dead run in the dark

No cowboy wanted to be caught in the middle of a stampede, a cattle herd's deadly mad dash to nowhere. So cowboys sang and whistled, watched for rustlers, and, when necessary, rode hard and fast to slow the herd.

Dangers stalked every cattle drive. In the early years, American Indians raided the drives to capture the horses. Cattle drives were slowed by blinding dust storms, wild prairie fires, dry watering holes, and the churning waters of flash floods. Stampedes, however, were the greatest danger on the trail. Cattle, especially Texas longhorns, were very nervous, and their huge horns were extremely dangerous. It took only a sudden, small noise or a fast movement to spook, or scare, them into blindly running in fear.

▲ Cowboys sometimes died on the trail, often trampled during a stampede. They were buried in shallow graves near the trail, and some of their grave markers can still be seen.

▼ Frederick Remington's painting *In a Stampede* showed a brave cowboy trying to control a stampede. He got the lead cattle to follow him as he turned into ever-smaller circles until they had no place to go and would stop.

▲ Cowboys wanted to be on a calm, well-trained horse when cattle took off at a run.

▲ Although any of the herd might start a stampede, the cattle would follow a lead steer if it slowed and stopped.

Calming nervous cattle

To keep the cattle calm at night, the cowboys whistled or sang as they rode night watch. It did not matter what they sang, because the steady sound of their voices calmed the cattle. But they usually sang about their loved ones or their hard lives. In 1910, John Lomax collected cowboy songs, including "The Jolly Rancher," which has this verse: "When threatening clouds do gather and herded lightnings flash, / And heavy rain drops splatter, and rolling thunders crash, / What keeps the herd from running, stampeding far and wide? / The cowboy's long, low whistle and singing by their side."

Dodge City: the most wicked town

Founded in 1872, Dodge City, Kansas, was the last and busiest Kansas cow town. Emanuel Dubbs, one of its earliest settlers, wrote in a 1909 book that "the name of Dodge City, Kansas, was known far and wide . . . The town grew almost in a night into a tented little city, every man was a law unto himself. In a few days 'Boot Hill' grave yard was started. At the approach of night the dance hall, saloons and gambling halls were a blaze of light and activity. The sharp report of the six-shooter became a nightly occurrence, and in the morning the usual question was: how many were killed last night?" Soon after it began, Dodge had 19 saloons and a gambling hall and was called one of the most wicked towns in the old West. This reputation lasted for ten years.

▶ Cowboys carried their guns in a holster, so it was easy to pull them out quickly.

Sharpshooting

Cowboys often passed the time practicing with their guns. They shot at targets such as rocks and plants. They needed to be a quick shot to kill the rattlesnakes that attacked them or to hunt for rabbits or antelope for their dinner. They held contests, sometimes against a professional shooter such as Annie Oakley.

▼ After law and order was introduced to Dodge City, gunfights broke out in only one part of town—where saloons, dance halls, and the gambling hall were allowed.

Changing the town's image

Dodge City had so many problems that the city hired Wyatt Earp to be the assistant marshal. This made many business owners unhappy, for they earned their living off the rowdy cowboys. Earp encouraged the town to divide into two parts along the railroad track. No guns were allowed on one side of the "deadline." On the other side, entertainment was provided for the cowboys.

Outlaws and Lawmen
Breaking the rules, keeping the peace

Violence and illegal activities made the West wild, but soon people began passing laws. To enforce the laws, they hired lawmen and sometimes went after outlaws on their own. Sometimes this led to more violence and deaths.

At first, people in cow towns did not enforce laws because they wanted to keep the cowboys happy. Then new settlers came with different ideas. They passed new laws and hired a lawman to "clean up" their town and enforce laws. In 1871, Abilene's new city government asked Wild Bill Hickok to be the town marshal, but those in charge soon found they did not like how he did the job. After only four years, Abilene was closed to cowboys and cattle. In 1892, Abilene businessman Charles Moreau Harger recalled in *Scribner's Magazine* "that might was the only law, and if . . . a marshal was found, like William Hickok, the original Wild Bill, who could rule an Abilene in its rudest period, it was because he was quicker with the revolver and more daring than even the cowboys themselves."

▼ Lawmen printed posters about the thieves and killers who were wanted—and the rewards given for those caught.

REWARD
☞ $10,000 ☜
IN GOLD COIN
Will be paid by the U. S. Government for the apprehension
DEAD OR ALIVE
of
SAM and BELLE STARR
Wanted for Robbery, Murder, Treason and other acts against the peace and dignity of the U. S.

THOMAS CRAIL

▶ The county sheriff's office and jail were often in the same room. A number of outlaws escaped from jail with help from their friends.

Gunfight at the OK Corral
In 1881, near the OK Corral in Tombstone, Arizona, the Clanton gang of cowboys, rustlers, and robbers fired on Wyatt Earp, his brothers, and Doc Holiday, who represented the law. In 30 seconds, about 30 bullets flew, killing three and injuring three.

▼ Sometimes a cowboy thought he was better than a famous lawman and would challenge the lawman to a gunfight.

The bad and the good
The most common outlaws were cattle rustlers. The worst worked in outlaw gangs, stealing many cattle, robbing banks or stagecoaches, and killing people. Lawmen, such as the Texas Rangers, sheriffs, and marshals, went after them. Also, ranchers joined together into cattlemen's associations to stop rustlers. The members might ride out themselves, as vigilantes, to find the rustlers or hire men who were good with a gun to do it. Vigilantes were people who took law enforcement into their own hands. They captured and punished those people they believed were killers or cattle rustlers without paying attention to the law.

Sometimes it was hard to tell the difference between an outlaw and a lawman. Men who were good with their guns were asked to become the sheriff, even if they had shot someone in an argument in another town. In 1936, lawman Elfego Baca told an interviewer about his days in western towns and said that he " . . . never wanted to kill anybody . . . but if a man had it in his mind to kill me, I made it my business to get him first."

▲ Legend says Billy the Kid killed 21 men, but he probably killed only four.

Fenced In, Forced Out

Dividing up the open range

Over time, the range became more crowded with farms, ranches, and cattle. Disagreements led to wars, and bad weather caused even more destruction. The cattle industry and cowboy life changed forever.

By 1890, ranchers had unofficially claimed much of the open range, while the government was selling the same land to farmers. Most cattle drives had ended because barbed-wire fences crossed trails and railroad stops were closer to ranches. Also, states had closed their borders to cattle drives, for they did not want the problems brought by cowboys or the disease and damage brought by Texas cattle.

Battles over the range

Barbed wire kept cattle off farm fields and on a ranch's grasslands. But more cattle grazed on less land, so the grass was eaten too fast and had no time to grow back. Battles broke out about land use, the causes of overgrazing, and fencing the range. Fences were cut, animals were destroyed, and people were killed.

In the late 1880s, farmer J. W. Hagerty watched barbed-wire fences going up in Texas: "Mr. Harpole had just about completed half of the fencing of his range when . . . men who were opposed to the fence organized a crew . . . the fence was destroyed . . . Harpole rebuilt the fence and [it] was guarded for about two weeks . . . it was again destroyed."

▲ Barbed wire is made of metal wire spikes stuck between twisted metal wires.

▲ A group of fence-cutters in Nebraska in 1900 disguise themselves from the photographer.

The Range Wars

In 1892, large ranchers in Johnson County, Wyoming, passed laws against small ranchers. They believed small ranchers were rustling cattle and causing overgrazing. The cattle barons hired gunmen and went after the men on their list. They attacked and burned one ranch but were trapped by 200 men at another. For two days, shots were fired. Then the governor asked for U.S. Army troops to break up the fighting and bring an end to the Johnson County War.

▲ In the Pleasant Valley Range War in Arizona in the 1880s, cattle ranchers fought with sheepherders and their supporters. Animals and people were killed.

Years of weather disasters

In the early 1880s, droughts—long periods with little or no rainfall—meant even less grass. The cattle became thin and weak. Then in 1885, blizzards hit the southern ranges. That spring, ranchers found thousands of dead cattle. Some surviving cattle were sent to the northern ranges to fatten up. The next winter, even stronger blizzards hit the northern ranches and lasted for months. Hundreds of thousands of cattle were found dead when spring finally arrived.

A changed cattle industry

Ranching and being a cowboy changed after the winter of 1886. Many ranches went out of business, and those left kept smaller herds on fenced land they owned or rented. Cowboys had to grow hay, repair windmills, and build and fix fences. A cowboy song of the time comparing the bad and good old days of the round-ups ended with the phrase (and was also titled) "The Camp-Fire Has Gone Out."

"The Great Die-up"

In the springs of 1886 and 1887, dead cattle were found packed together along barbed-wire fences as if trying to stay warm in the winter storms.

▼ During the winter the cowboys brought hay to the cattle and pulled out those trapped in the snow.

▼ When settlers built farms, they sometimes ignored the trails, so cattle wandered near their homes and trampled their fields. Farmers helped pass laws to stop the cattle drives from coming near.

ONE OF OUR ROSEBUD SWELL FORK STOCK SADDLES, $21.99

OUR "JEFFERSON" IMPROVED SADDLE STOCK $26.99

$27.50

$30.59

$23.59

$15.37

$26.99

$21.19

$27.99

▲ The Sears mail-order catalog showed the cowboys versions of items they needed, such as saddles. The cowboys sometimes papered their bunkhouse with pages from the catalog so they had something to read over the long winter.

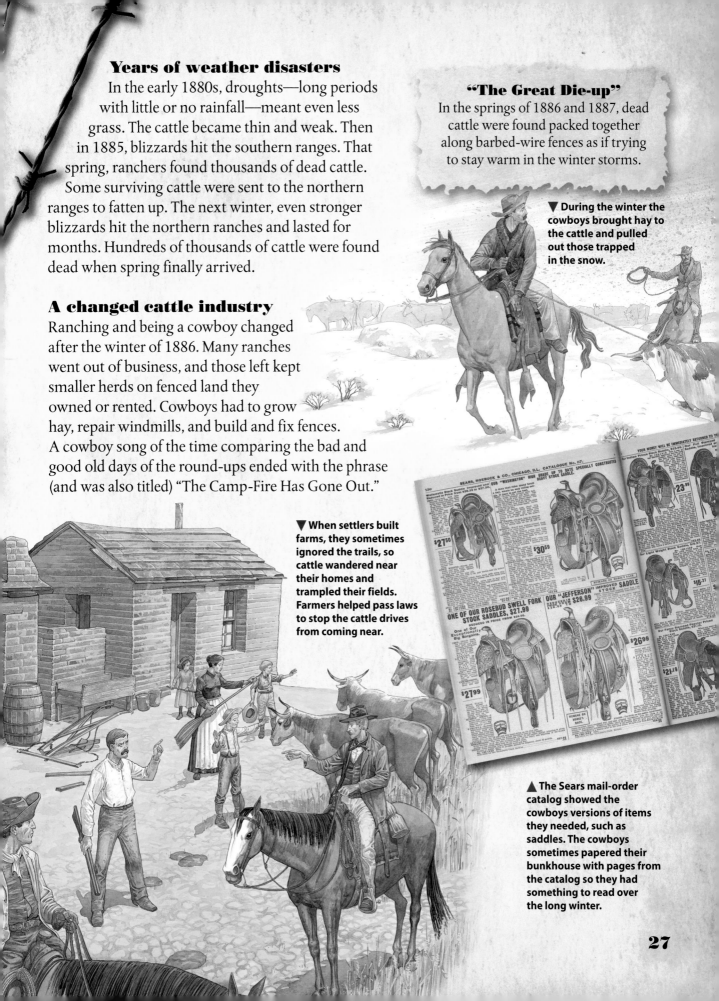

The End of an Era

From cattle herders to movie stars

As the golden age of cowboys, cow towns, and cattle drives came to an end, the legend of the West and the people who had lived there continued to grow. The legend was fed, and still is, by new books, Wild West shows, paintings, and movies.

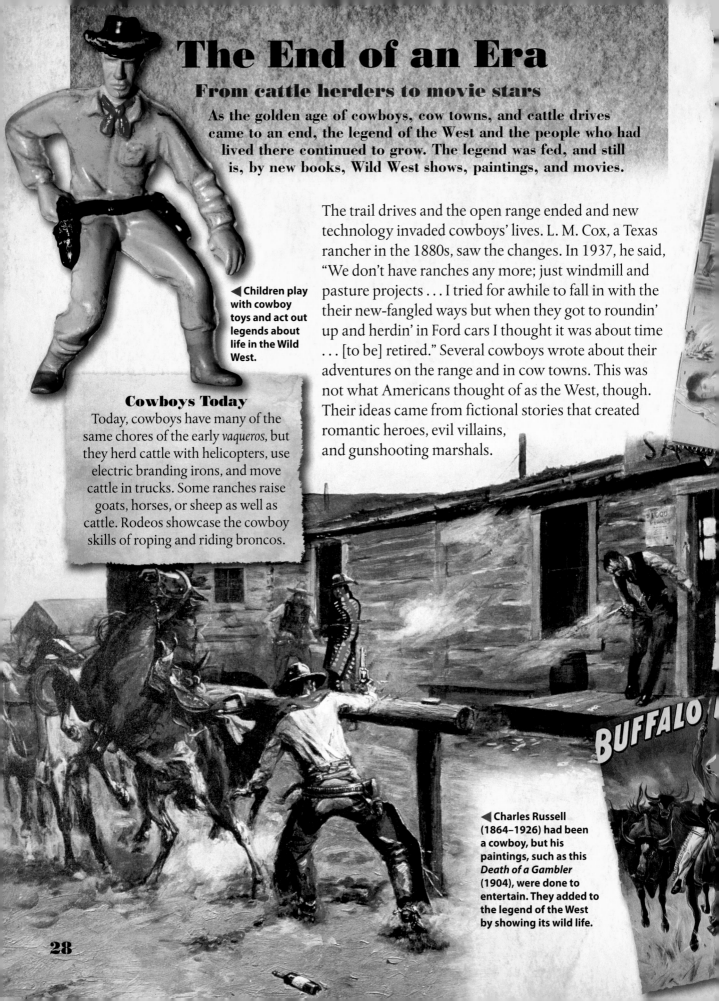

◀ Children play with cowboy toys and act out legends about life in the Wild West.

Cowboys Today

Today, cowboys have many of the same chores of the early *vaqueros*, but they herd cattle with helicopters, use electric branding irons, and move cattle in trucks. Some ranches raise goats, horses, or sheep as well as cattle. Rodeos showcase the cowboy skills of roping and riding broncos.

The trail drives and the open range ended and new technology invaded cowboys' lives. L. M. Cox, a Texas rancher in the 1880s, saw the changes. In 1937, he said, "We don't have ranches any more; just windmill and pasture projects . . . I tried for awhile to fall in with the their new-fangled ways but when they got to roundin' up and herdin' in Ford cars I thought it was about time . . . [to be] retired." Several cowboys wrote about their adventures on the range and in cow towns. This was not what Americans thought of as the West, though. Their ideas came from fictional stories that created romantic heroes, evil villains, and gunshooting marshals.

◀ Charles Russell (1864–1926) had been a cowboy, but his paintings, such as this *Death of a Gambler* (1904), were done to entertain. They added to the legend of the West by showing its wild life.

28